HIP LOGIC

TERRANCE HAYES was the recipient of a Whiting Writers Award and the Kate Tufts Discovery Award for *Muscular Music*, his debut collection of poems. He was born in Columbia, South Carolina and holds degrees from Coker College, where he studied painting and English, and the University of Pittsburgh, where he studied poetry. His work has appeared in numerous literary journals and anthologies of emerging writers, including *American poetry: The Next Generation* and *Giant Steps: The New Generation of African American Writers*. He teaches in the Creative Writing Department at Carnegie Mellon University and lives in Pittsburgh, Pennsylvania, with his wife and daughter.

THE NATIONAL POETRY SERIES

The National Poetry Series was established in 1978 to ensure the publication of five poetry books annually through participating publishers. Publication is funded by the late James A. Michener, the Copernicus Society of America, Edward J. Piszek, the Lannan Foundation, the National Endowment for the Arts, and the Tiny Tiger Foundation.

2001 COMPETITION WINNERS

BETSY BROWN of Minnesota, *Year of Morphines*
Chosen by George Garrett, to be published by Louisiana State University Press

DAVID GROFF of New York, *Theory of Devolution*
Chosen by Mark Doty, to be published by University of Illinois Press

TERRANCE HAYES of Pennsylvania, *Hip Logic*
Chosen by Cornelius Eady, to be published by Viking Penguin

ELIZABETH ROBINSON of California, *Pure Descent*
Chosen by Fanny Howe, to be published by Sun & Moon Press

RUTH L. SCHWARTZ of California, *Edgewater*
Chosen by Jane Hirshfield, to be published by HarperCollins Publishers

TERRANCE HAYES

Hip Logic

PENGUIN BOOKS
Published by the Penguin Group
Penguin Group (USA) Inc., 375 Hudson Street, New York, New York 10014, U.S.A.
Penguin Books Ltd, 80 Strand, London WC2R 0RL, England
Penguin Books Australia Ltd, 250 Camberwell Road, Camberwell, Victoria 3124, Australia
Penguin Books Canada Ltd, 10 Alcorn Avenue, Toronto, Ontario, Canada M4V 3B2
Penguin Books India (P) Ltd, 11 Community Centre, Panchsheel Park, New Delhi – 110 017, India
Penguin Group (NZ), cnr Airborne and Rosedale Roads, Albany, Auckland 1310, New Zealand
Penguin Books (South Africa) (Pty) Ltd, 24 Sturdee Avenue,
Rosebank, Johannesburg 2196, South Africa

Penguin Books Ltd, Registered Offices: 80 Strand, London WC2R 0RL, England

First published in Penguin Books 2002

12 14 16 18 20 19 17 15 13 11

LIBRARY OF CONGRESS CATALOGING IN PUBLICATION DATA
Hayes, Terrance.
    Hip logic / Terrance Hayes.
        p. cm.—(National poetry series)
    ISBN 0-14-200139-2
    I. Title. II. Series.

PS3558.A8378 H57 2002
811'.54—dc21
                        2002020871

Printed in the United States of America
Set in Universe Condensed
Designed by M. Paul

For Yona and Ua, my points of Light

"Please," he said.

TABLE OF CONTENTS

III. Conjure

IV. A Gram of &s

V. The Law of Falling & Catching Up

Hip Logic

LORDE

Walking our boundaries
We arrived at my mother's island

We entered silence

We have no passions left to love
We were born in a poor time

What am I ready to lose
What anger in my hard-won bones

What hues lie in the slit
When a mask breaks
When love leaps from my mouth

Who are you
Without expectation

I. At the First Clear Word

emcee

You get to wear triple X
Jeans for easy access to the lair of first breaths

You get to reveal your shank
Handmade with the tooth of a bed spring and gauze

You get to rhyme about death—

Explicit lyrics, you are the pied piper
Sending children into jerk patterns and grunts
Into tunnels of smoke—

I had to get high to write this—

Your mind twists,
Gleams like lights on the bends of a night-coaster
The riders throw their hands in the air—

You get Grandmaster mantras—
And wave 'em like they just don't care

Under your spell I can do anything

Fly girls and Hoochie Mommas, La Femme Fantabulous
Writing your phone number on their tongues

Sucka emcees can call me Sire

Indelible tattoos
The night cut on an open sentence—
You are the Alpha and the Omegaphone

The night cut and you won't ever be alone—
Your grin of gold-plated windows

You want the exit code from the tenement, the penitentiary—
You want [beatbox   beatbox   beatbox]

Breathlessness

TOUCH

We made our own laws.
I want to be a Hawk,
A Dolphin, a Lion, we'd say

In stores where team logos hung
Like animal skins.

By moonlight,
We chased each other
Around the big field

Beneath branches sagging
As if their leaves were full of blood.

We didn't notice when policemen
Came lighting tree bark
& our skin with flashlights.

They saw our game
For what it was:

Fingers clutching torso,
Shoulder, wrist—a brawl.
Some of the boys escaped,

Their brown legs cut by thorns
As they ran through the brush.

It's true, we could have been mistaken
For animals in the dark,
But of all our possible crimes,

Blackness was the first.
So they tackled me,

And read me my rights without saying:
You Down or *Dead Ball*.
We had a language

They did not use, a name
For collision. We called it Touch.

THE THINGS-NO-ONE-KNOWS BLUES
—after Wanda Coleman

I filed for bankruptcy in the borough of luxury.
I suspect it's time to eat my poetry.
My favorite turtleneck sweater, the green,
50% rayon, 5% cotton (rest unknown) one,

shrank in a tub of hot
bath water. A prisoner bit
a chunk out of my step-daddy's smile.
My mamma filled

her cancer with silicone
& pity. My wife dwells in
a house of critics. I'm younger than
sugar, but older than

NutraSweet because I had a birthday in
New Orleans.
I suffer various degrees
of wistfulness.

Honey,
I guess it's time I eat my poetry.
Cranked to ten my Walkman screams
static. I believe B.B. fingered

Lucille like the back of a pretty woman's knee,
but no one seems to agree.
Need pecks at the latch
of my Wal-Mart wristwatch.

The lines on my palms slope like portable ex
& why graphs. Baby, I suffer various degrees of wistfulness.
I suspect my penis will
be fed to a swimming Gila

monster. Occasionally Death
calls me collect.

ARS POETICA # 789

My daddies have voices
like bachelors, like castigators & crooners.
They have busted kneecaps.
They stand behind my mother
in the kitchen pretending to count the hairs
on her neck. One of my daddies
was a carpenter. One lost his tooth
in a fistfight with Jesus. One went to prison.
No, two went to prison. One daddy sits beside me
telling jokes dull as mouthwash.
One can guess how many catfish swim
in every pond. Here is my scar
from a summer working in the glass factory
across from another daddy's home.
My daddy with the pretty gold-tooth smile taps
my shoulder & says, "Look at the booty
on that gal." My daddy, Mr. Blacker-than-most,
wears shades in the house. He says
"Nobody's blacker than me, Boy."
Each of my daddies asks, "Are you writing
another poem about me?" They covet secrets.
No, my daddies covet work above secrets.
We are watching an action movie now,
my daddies & me. There are guns & damsels
& camouflage. There are car wrecks
& cusswords & blood. But my daddies are tired.
Some of them sprawl on the carpet.
Some of them go upstairs to the bedrooms,
or through the front door to the porch.
My daddies fall asleep in all the rooms
inside & outside the house. I want to sleep too,
but their snores make the wind chimes tremble.

HIP LOGIC

Some shoot the soft bloodless
heads of basketballs. Shoes filled
with darkness. Skulls & dragons
stitched into biceps.
No standing still.
Some cruise with detachable faces
on their radios. The grief latent
in speed limits & zip codes.
The evening between evenings.
Stalls with locked doors.
Some leave their car windows
cracked & a boomboomboom
rustles the neighborhood.
No standing still. The law says
no stone will go uncrushed.
It won't make the news.
Some will be set free for lack
of evidence or imprisoned
despite it. Trying to catch
the soul here? Like trying
to slow light down to a trot.
Some dress in women's arms.
Perpetually groomed & grooming.
Hips are the cradle of logic.
Sperm hop in the trenches
blessed with an ageless memory.

SONNET

We sliced the watermelon into smiles.
We sliced the watermelon into smiles.
We sliced the watermelon into smiles.
We sliced the watermelon into smiles.
We sliced the watermelon into smiles.
We sliced the watermelon into smiles.
We sliced the watermelon into smiles.
We sliced the watermelon into smiles.
We sliced the watermelon into smiles.
We sliced the watermelon into smiles.
We sliced the watermelon into smiles.
We sliced the watermelon into smiles.
We sliced the watermelon into smiles.
We sliced the watermelon into smiles.

MR. T—

A man made of scrap muscle & the steam
engine's imagination, white feathers
flapping in each lobe for the skull's migration,
should the need arise. Sometimes drugged
& duffled (by white men) in a cockpit
bound for the next adventure. And liable
to crush a fool's face like newsprint; headlines
of Hollywood blood and wincing. Half Step 'N Fetchit,
half John Henry. What were we, the skinny B-boys,
to learn from him? How to hulk through Chicago
in a hedgerow afro, an ox-grunt kicking dust
behind the teeth; those eighteen glammering
gold chains around the throat of pity,
that fat hollow medallion like the sun on a leash—

SHAFT & THE ENCHANTED SHOE FACTORY
or
ARS POETICA: THE EPIC QUEST FOR LANGUAGE

Shoeboxes line the walls like books.
Shaft sits alone untying his boots.

He's Jesse-Owened across Harlem in these shoes,
He's tossed them like a pair of guns
By the beds of countless women,
He's kicked down the doors of villains.

But now they are scarred as a pair of old boxing gloves
The leather too thin to protect his strut through Broadway slush.

Suddenly, a long man in a blue satin robe appears,
His fingers thin as calligraphy pens.
He's the factory wizard,
Distant cousin some mythic shoemaker god,
Provider of footwear
For every hero in the land:
Blue suede for Elvis,
Snakeskin spur-spinning boots for John Wayne,
Red boots for Superman.

Shaft says, *Man I'm about to walk from Chicago to Mississippi*
Kicking the ass of every redneck & Republican that moves,

I'm about to slow drag with a woman finer than Nefertiti,
And soon as she starts to love me, I'm gonna leave her with the blues...

The rest of the shit I'm planning is none of your business,
I'm here looking for new shoes.

The wizard grins a cascade of teeth,
& pulls a pair of tap-dance shoes out of his cuff.
But how can you sneak into a bad guy's hideout
In loud-ass Sammy-Davis-Jr. kicks?
Is what Shaft's thinking. The wizard reads his mind.

He unveils a pair of steel-toe boots.
Shaft's father was a construction worker.
At the end of his life, he had ten exquisite toes,
But the work curled his spine.
Shaft says nothing but the wizard can read his mind.

He pulls out Bo Jacksons, then Air Jordans,
Then clogs, moccasins, house slippers, ballerina shoes.
Shaft says, *Ahh Man, fuck this shit, I'm about to go.*

The wizard raises his arms to cast a spell
Called Hocus Pocus Jim Crow.
Shaft frowns & says *Man you go to Hell.*
& Jim-Kellys him through a wall of wing tips with his five big toes.

Shaft returns his feet to his old boots
And his soles and ankles thank him.
The dazed wizard groans beneath a yellow halo of canaries.
Theme music blasts as Shaft walks out into a ticker tape of snow.

SQUAWK

Under the spell
Of the doctor's blue polka-dot sweater,
Big Bird revealed the horrors of his life.
His love had always been easy,
He'd left lush clouds & Florida vacations
To teach us goodness & the alphabet,
He'd spent nights dreaming of swans
& feathering a lonely erection.

> "I only wanted to be a bird like any other bird,
> I used to wander flock to flock but found
> the chirpish love any star receives from fans.
> When I showed up at dinner parties,
> the guests whispered: Who invited the bird?
> They giggled at my yellow afro, my Jewish beak.
>
> Look at me!
> King of the Muppet rejects:
> Oscar & his can of rust & sour trash,
> The Cookie Monster & his greedy Negro mumble,
> Bert & Ernie the secret lovers, Kermit,
> the Unenchanted frog!
> We've spent our lives making you laugh,
> and I'm tired of it,
> tired of this prison of make-believe!"

He began tearing at himself.
Feathers flew.

The doctor sneezed & his sweater dazzled.
Big Bird yanked til his skin was uncovered,
Twisted til his big head popped off,
And when the yellow cloud settled,

Only a tiny black man remained.
Tears fluttered from his eyes & he sang,
Freeeee! I'm free at last.

Meanwhile, the doctor tugged
A magic button on his magic sweater,
And a giant rushed in carrying a straightjacket
—a big yellow-feathered straightjacket.

Somewhere Tweety was being eaten by a cat;
The Road Runner was running out of road.
The black man ruffled & squawked with rage.

BUTTER

The same old dream: women of the globe on a love strike. They want equal rights. Power. At first the men don't believe the threat. They're content to only hug their dates. Walk on the beach, even. Content to drive home unsexed. Maybe tomorrow. All the men think, Maybe tomorrow she'll invite me in. A little talk. A little skin, tomorrow.

Then, one by one, they figure it out. No more sex. They realize it squinting over Penthouse Pets, Playboy Bunnies and old porno of fine retired starlets. They know it fisting themselves in wee hours while wives sleep, tight-lipped, beside them.

But power is better than sex, say congressmen and athletes and movie idols. And power is better than tiny infants whining like sirens. This is what they decide.

Years later, after the women have moved North to little towns in breast-shaped hills, the men are so desperate they have slumber parties and hug each other. Mushy, I know—but true. The women live an arm's length from the lowest star, and way down in the valley below, the men ration love like bits of metal in wartime. Mope around with sunken heads, chests flat as tin. It's true. They have eyes dark and vacant as closets without dresses.

Meanwhile the ladies live in big houses made of chocolate. Mirrors in every room. Music all the time. But it's also true, the women are lonely. Nights they wander in front of mirrors, room to chocolate room sulking in hot, unhandled skin. Very, very sad indeed. Soon there are no children in the land. Everyone lives alone and dreams of what could fill it: the space between absence.

You're waiting for the part that saves them. Aphrodite entering the land one day. A woman old as fire, but creaseless. Eleven fertile organs. Yes, I want to tell you she came when the world was at the end of its rope. Laid down like a shiny fish for the stupid ravenous men.

But she didn't. Instead the men grew bitter. Decided to ride their Jeeps to the hills and murder the righteous women—but wait, men could never be so brutal. I'm sure. So maybe it was butter. The men grew butter at the center of each sorrowed, milky heart, and sent it up the mountain to the women.

The women were perplexed (Butter?), but accepted the gift. Next morning a truckload of them rode down to the town where men lay tugging their cocks like umbilical roots; hoping sperm would tadpole to babies in their loins.

The women rode into town with the pounds of butter. In the streets they rubbed it on themselves. Ecstatic men ran out and embraced them. Then they all ate until each belly was pregnant with gratitude. Until butter sang like light on their lips. Yes this is true. But what does it mean? Did the women finally get their demands? Use butter as a reminder of each man's golden promise to equality? Or was it a trap? Did the men eat all the women and later die with cholesterol jammed like scorn in their hearts? Who knows?

    In the morning I'll slide butter on my lover's toast.

ORIGIN OF THE DAYS

SUNDAY: day of sun, a word old as religion.
the fishermen lean their rods
among broomsticks & boat oars,
slap rough hands together & pray
nonfishermen will die.
Also: the iridescent furious & something filial.

MONDAY: from the prefix, mono. Alone. Single. One.
Also mononucleosis, after kissing a fish with one mouth.
Also: day of the moon when the O is shuffled or eclipsed.
Also: *moan* day as the week begins to unpeel again:
the bed moans, the bones moan.

TUESDAY: for pairs. Shoes. Feet. Legs.
For courtship: Two eyes that see differently:
Left eye says, The moon is like a skull.
Right eye says, The moon is like an egg.
Also, of course, for the number 2 day.
Also for immediacy as in, I love you 2day & 2morrow we wed.

WEDNESDAY: Behold! the wedding of the weekdays.
Tuesday stitched to Thursday.
Also derived from wedge.
As in something that serves to split, part, divide.

THURSDAY: as in thors day or thornsday
meaning the hammer god will save us from the roses,
the crude love left over from Wednesday.
Also: Thirstday. Meaning I cannot afford a drink until payday.

FRIDAY: Fishfry day. Some fish on your plate.
Breaded skin & fish heads gawking from the trash.
"Fish!" your father says, "Men fish!"
Meaning you are not a man,
if you don't work & writing is not work.
Your tongue is a fish out of water.
You nearly die of thirst.

SATURDAY: for the god of farms & a haloed planet.
Also for evenings on the town: a lady's satin
evening gown, the nightclub sashay.
But mostly for satellite t.v. As in a satchel full of time.
As in stars. As in saturnine. Meaning, I just sat
on the dock of the bed all day.

GOSPEL OF THE TWO SISTERS
—after Tony Hoagland

Long ago two sisters lived in a small brick house beside a super highway. The tall chatty one knew the first & last name of every animal in the galaxy. The small quiet one could make her hair grow longer or shorter with no more than a thought.

The pecan-colored sister said, "I wish I had the shiny exoskeleton of the *Monomorium Minimum*," & when the penny-colored sister squinted her eyes, hair spilled across the floors & they had carpet.

But the girls had no other relatives or friends & eventually they grew sick of each other. One day the sister with the gold hoop earrings said, the mastiff, a large, powerful, short-haired dog is ancestor of the pit bull, the boxer, & the Saint Bernard, but it is the ugliest breed of them all & then, after a few unusual moments of silence, said: "Sister, do you ever wished we had a mother to braid our hair?"

The sister with the banana-colored Bruce Lee-press on nails rolled her eyes & though she was stone-faced, her hair began to weep & she looked suddenly like someone who'd been walking in the rain.

I can remember how I came to believe in God. I was sitting one Sunday in the front row listening to three dirt-old deacons sing an acappella "Amazing Grace" when a trembling like fingers through a tub of water passed through me. I opened my mouth & remembered the time my cousin Junebug held me in the Sleeper Hold until I blacked out.

For many years afterward the sister that could sprint eighty miles without stopping paced up & down the hallway waiting for the right sentence to worm into her ear or push out of her mouth & the sister that could sleep underwater sat in a rocking chair awaiting the same thing.

Then the sisters discovered they were pregnant & each gave birth to a boy on the same dry September day. The sister with the tattoo of Joe Frazier bought every bit of baby blue in the city & countryside for her son & dressed him in a new outfit twice an hour. The sister with eyes like two bowls of black bean soup bought every children's book ever written, & began reading them nonstop as soon as her son grew ears.

The sons said they just wanted music.

How often do you hear the tenderness you need to hear? I mean exactly when you need to hear it? Is it ever before that little yolk of hurt wraps itself in layers hard enough to break teeth?

The sister with the overbite asked the sister with bullet in her hip, "Do we even remember how to sing? "They had not spoken to each other in several years so they'd forgotten the sound words made fluttering between them. Then the son with the bucket head smiled at the son with elephant ears & the sisters' scratchy, awkward gospel began to unravel & crawl across the room.

II. A Gram of &s

a b d u c t o r

Because I cannot correct my name. Because the boat
docks each night in the bay & the board-

walk creaks beneath women eager to tour
their dreams. Because I cannot court
the maiden. I am the actor

without a face. In a few seconds I will doubt
your love. I will spill vodka on the birthday card,
the wedding gloves. Because I cannot cart

the goodness from door to door, nor wait on the curb
of bad intentions. Because I cannot coat

my tongue in whispers, I take to the road.

a l t h o u g h

In spite of & otherwise. The way you halt.

The notwithstanding. The hula-
hoop of albeits. The way you haul
doubt around, your smile on auto-
pilot, the Halo-
maker's laugh
thundering above you. The way you ought
to go but fail to. The oath
you were told to take. The can'ts & thou
shan'ts declared by your Lord-In-A-Toga.

The way more & more, He begins to gloat.

a m b u l a n c e

Some fool ignores the manual
       Accompanying his sparkling ACME
Chainsaw. Or maybe someone orders spoiled cube
       Steak from a diner menu.
Or can't refuse his twelfth shot of *Jim Beam*.
       Whatever the case, those who balance
Mercy on a gurney of red & blue
       Light will come to the rescue. One medic able
To juggle bags of blood while his partner zigzags the fast lane.
       The ghosts of your grandparents will lean
Above you asking your name, but you won't have a clue.

a p o t h e c a r y

Where we're told they
House the Panacea Theory.
Where they get inside the mystery ache
& prescribe a therapy
That needs no pray-
Er. You'd like to be indestructible like the roach
So you follow the path
To the one some say will be able to hector
Your despair. Or at least take care
Of the dry patch
Of skin around your heart.

b e c k o n e d

Has your memory ever been
an unfenced county? A bend
in the road? I was down on one knee
forging a bond
with an unlucky leprechaun. I said *Bring the Eden
of first love here!* Suddenly, my neck
was leeched with hickeys. The keen
finger of a ghost clacked down my backbone
& I was lost in the district of need.
I'd known the way home once,
but now the past had its own area code.

b o w l i n g

"He got home late & ling-
ered in the kitchen & when I heard his wing-
tips shuffling down the hall, I imagined a lion
entering the bedroom. I lit a candle & began to glow.
I was in the same fire-pink gown
I wore on our wedding night. The one I won playing bingo.
I said, *Let's not talk about those glib*
pins at the edge of a lane & stretched as his long
fold-out fingers approached. But when he asked me to blow
on his chicken noodle soup to cool it down, my sweat began to boil!
Yes, I threw the soup on him, Your Honor. Then I threw the bowl."

b r e a t h e

When my great-great-grandfather Caesar plops out of the ether
in the middle of my Saturday evening bath,
I gasp not because I hate
seeing naked old phantoms, but because he begins to heat
the water way beyond a degree I can bear!
(If you are 135, give or take a decade, you have no business visiting earth.)
And what an effort to convince him to beat
it! He soaps a corner of the cage around his heart
& with an expression promising, but distant as a mail-in rebate,
tells me he only intends to stay here
until he can find a room to rent at an affordable rate.

careless

Dear Self, yesterday after class
I saw a man who was a slightly used, large scale
version of you. I watched him ease
the city bus through an acre
of traffic on the south side. He said to a crass
young boy who apparently thought recess
was a full-time job: "Son. Son, please cease
propping your feet on my seats." Wasn't your daddy's real
name Butch? Look, maybe you don't care,
but this dude even had the same facial scar
as you. It was your father. Couldn't have been anyone else.

c o r p o r a l

Best known in youth for its punishments, its poor
Grasps at pleasure. As in fantasies of dates where chocolate & cola
Do not later overrun the face with a crop
Of pimples. It is the simple, but loco
Motives. As in creeping through evening snow to croon a carol
At a girl's window. It is not singing, but a roar
That does not cease. The stench of imitation Polo
Cologne on the breeze. It is shoveling coal
Into the heart's mindless furnace. The lack of cool.
The skin's burning color.
The skull's charred parlor.

example

An instance made of little moments. *Huh?* Consider the lamp
which has no shade. *A lamp, Master?* Or the palm
covering a crotch that could be better covered by a maple
leaf. *Master, I don't understand.* Sometimes, when you peel
back the bright wrapper of Metaphor, there is nothing but a lame
blank below. *I—? What do you mean?* Even at the apex
of your WISDOM there will be exam
questions, whole riddles, you do not know. [silence.] I wish you no male-
dictions, Disciple, but the time will come to cop a plea.
But what about Wisdom? Yes, make the S into an N; spin the M on its axle
& you will get a WINDOW. *What?* But beware: no one will catch you when you leap.

III. Conjure

III. Conjure

FRIDAY POEM
Japan, 1998

I ascend a few steps behind the women
because passion sometimes climbs a ladder
over the fence of good sense. *Sexual Healing*
is humping into my earphones.
I have a box of lemon tea a woman sold me
saying: "*Takai*," meaning: "I am tall," "You are tall,"
"They are tall" in a language without pronouns.
I think she was flirting. There's no escaping
Spring's drug. A young man will take an escalator
to the scalp of a ten-story building
lured by petals of a skirt, the scent of wonder.
He will enter the rooftop museum
because the walls are covered with women
painted in the name of what consumes him.
At the center of each nude,
a tiny pulpit where logic kneels in prayer.
You can tell what's important to a culture
by the size of its buildings. In America
the superstadiums swell & dazzle
even astronomers on Mars. In Japan
the shopping stores are grand towers
packed with single women & housewives.
In my city the buildings are tall as the spine's
supple steeple & men drag ladders
through the streets. How else can I explain
what I did with Friday? I listened
to Marvin croon something sexual
to the point of despair. I sat in the museum
like a monk who, after many days lost
without water, finds a woman bathing in a creek.

FOR PAUL ROBESON

Ol' Man River, he don't say nothin', He must know somethin'. . .

They have never heard a voice deeper
Than mud at the bottom of a bottomless creek
They have never heard gospel or the blood's spirit speak
They have never heard a storm come down & break
The river free, they have never seen the river break free
They have never seen a stone turn the temple to meat
They have never seen a mother in flames or a funeral wreath
They have never seen a black man weep
Dear Paul, they come each night to the Opera house-seats
They have never heard a voice so deep
They have never heard the sound when a river breaks free

DIEGO RIVERA—*DAMA DE BLANCO*, 1939

Cobwebs & mandrake. Bride holding the skull
of her husband. When Diego said, *Where is the gown
you wore at the wedding*, she wept pulling it from a trunk.
But it was the color he wanted. The white of skirts
on flower vendors. Of calla lilies. She knows
Diego makes love to all the women he paints,
even Frida's sister. (What color is the line
between greed & passion?) When Diego asks,
will she lift the gown & sprawl like a puddle of light,
the brush dragging a silver trail along her thigh?
Will the skull rolling into the hall sound
like a moaning man? This afternoon in the museum,
among cobwebs & a plant that screams when pulled
from the ground, she smiles as if her secret is a good one.
This we learn is how to be a bride with no husband,
how to hold a skull upon the lap like a purse
of freedom. In 1939, she smiles at Diego, his gut large
enough to hold a harem of skulls, a woman-sized fetus.
(She has seen Frida walking to the market
in his shadow.) Her smile is a wall rising out of his colors,
beauty he swallows then returns, ruins then restores . . .

FOR ROBERT HAYDEN

Did your father come home after fighting
through the week at work? Did the sweat change
to salt in his ears? Was that bitter white

grain the only music he'd hear? Is this why
you were quiet when other poets sang
of the black man's beauty? Is this why

you choked on the tonsil of Negro Duty?
Were there as many offices for pain
as love? Should a black man never be shy?

Was your father a mountain twenty
shovels couldn't bury? Was he a train
leaving a lone column of smoke? Was he

a black magnolia singing at your feet?
Was he a blackjack smashed against your throat?

BROKEN DANGERFIELD NEWBY VILLANELLE

My voice made them shiver;
My voice called starlings from the trees
So a farmer pried loose my teeth

And stomped them into the dirt.
But I heard what I could not speak:
Gasps, a dog barking, a church bell.

They said shit hung from my lips;
They said my mouth was full of piss.
A carpenter sawed off my ears,

But I saw what I could not hear:
Boot strings, a church steeple, houseflies.
A butcher pried loose my eyes

And crushed them in his fist.
But I thought what I could not see:
My wife somewhere cradling our child.

A blacksmith cracked open my skull
And scooped my memory from its shell.
But I sensed my own beauty;
What I could not remember, I felt—

WILLIAM H. JOHNSON
—a letter home, circa 1933

Forgive this letter covered in paint.
There are no rags around me.
I cannot tell you where I am, but where I ain't.

I am not where the color of my skin taints
Everything. Remember the way folks looked at me
When I walked through Florence covered in paint?

There, I was less than nothing. I took a train
To Harlem; a ship to Denmark to be free.
I can only tell you that here, I ain't

Who I used to be. I am a Negro who has lain
With a white woman in a foreign country.
Momma, forgive this letter covered in paint.

I ain't coming back. Here, no one complains
When Holcha & I kiss in the street.
Color doesn't tells us what we are & what we ain't

Never going to be. I have left my name
On the walls of a dozen museums & galleries.
I have covered my face in paint.
I cannot tell you who I am, but who I ain't.

ODE TO BALTHUS

Old dirty, dirty. Old dirty, dirty handful of skin & motion.
There is a girl in white and girl in green & red and girl in nothing
And each is walking away. Handful of crimson ribbon
Pulled from hair tangled like rain around a girl's face.
Handful of blood & bliss and the pain of blood & bliss.
How long before their fingers curl into questions
Deadly as the scorpion's tail? The studio filled with a virgin's
Ruined smell. Old dirty, dirty handful of light & space.
Girl sprawled on a couch, a girl on a horse, girl in a mirror.
The orchid's tender stem in a hipped-shaped vase.

"THE GULF STREAM" / FOUR STUDIES

I. Homer / Apparition

then my dream went black   as a sea   without borders

I'd seen the back of a woman   waiting on a pier
           in a blood red shawl

      she'd found my dozen sketches
of the young half-naked Negro   tether-veined   thick-necked
        his scowl   looking away

a vision   so foreign she left my house
        & ran until the tide took her in

     a blackness finally   she nor I could possess

in the dream   I'd been ready to hold him
        to stroke   a thin line out of nothing

I wanted to give him the brave & tender   loneliness
     of the sea   he was going to tell me
what the world was like   without sun

but my brush fell   my dream went black
    & I could not make him   swim out of death

II. Fishmonger / Libation

To the gasp,
       the murmur and swell.

To the premonition
       that becomes a wound.

To the narrow path
       that leads from everything.

To the fishmongers who live,
       to the green mermaid tattoos
covering their scars.

To the fishmongers' wives,
       grateful
even when their men return
       with empty nets.

(How will my family survive?
       How will my boat be found?)

To the snapped mast.
       To the sunken prow.

To the blue blue
       and each fin and tooth.

To the glimmer of salt
       on the skin.

To the scent of drifting,
       the rock & sway.

To the tide's radiance
       unwiring the tongue.

A toast
       to this long-standing rain
this holy water,
       to this poisoned wine

I drink.

III. The Sea / Temptation

Let me varnish your bones,
     Let me dress them in salt;
a thousand years of rain

covering fortune; your bed
     & heaven, both halves
of the distance from home.

Let me varnish them blue
     & brush them with salt
as a lover should do.

Leagues of stars have fallen
     against me;
a procession of lovesick moons.

I am a willful woman
     walking to church
in black shoes,

The one who can bend
     the coast;
the one who can juggle

storms & pearls
     in a mouth
that will never grow old.

Let me tell you the legend
     of the widow whose tears
filled seven valleys.

Let me varnish your bones.
    I know of a room
where no hours are kept.

Let me dress them in salt.
    Let me fill you with a bounty
more enduring than breath.

IV. Self Portrait / Vision

The man tells nothing. He carries nothing,
   He is covered by almost nothing,
      But strokes of light.

He knows what I would like to know:
How a white man came to paint beauty
      Into a black man's face,
& why he left sharks slashing the water below his feet?

But he does say.
   I am not his kin. I, who was born
Of a people who never learned to swim,
      People who had no word
For the blue line that divides each day;
   This is why he does not look my way.

So we pine for his never-minding scowl:
Homer at his easel in 1899,
      As the harbor filled with saltwater & lightning;
& me these last months
      I've spent staring at the painting
As rain & wind walked hand in hand into this city.

Did he know it would storm that day,
   This mariner or fishmonger,
      This refugee backtracking
Through the Middle Passage,
   Kingdom of the unsalvaged, the hushed fathoms;
Fleeing home to find home?

I can pretend, but I do not know enough.
Or I know as much as Homer could have known
            Of what a drowned man feels:

        The flood of last wishes;
    & the hours beginning
                To darken & drift off course.

As a child I'd sneak to watch teenagers
    Roughneck in the neighborhood pool.

One night as I knelt at the deep end
    Stroking the water,
            A white boy shoved me in.

Can you remember the womb?
            How, in the moments before birth,
The lines were washed from the map
    That told the route you'd come?
Perhaps drowning feels that way.

The one who saved me had dark skin.
He left me on my side
    Gasping for air like a startled fish.

After my father removed my soaked shirt & sneakers,
            He got his belt.
He beat me until welts rose
    Like new muscles along my arms & legs;
Like brushstrokes along my back.

I learned living requires a kind of discipline;
   A reverence for the law of gravity.

But I have wanted,
      As I want when I look at the painting,
         To unhouse my body.

I have wanted the kind of grace God gives
      Only to the drowned;
         The boundlessness

Of a man conjured
      Out of gossip & time,
Out of theories of demise;

Of a man who will not be the painter's handsome one,
Who does not ask for help,
           But awaits the tide's eulogy.

SLEEPING WOMAN

so close that your hand on my chest is my hand
so close that your eyes close as I fall asleep.
—Pablo Neruda

Yes, cigarettes are metaphors for sex or solitude itself;
whatever is live and deep and gone. We stood
in the express lane with Parliaments, our last dollars
crumpled in my palm. I have always been
a left-handed man, meaning a dumb passion crashes
through my brain, requesting everything I have and have not.
This hand is what I have left. I'm talking about control
or lacking it. We should have bought bread,
but I bought smoke. Now, you have fallen asleep,
And I am lifting the last of a solitary butt to my lips.
In photos Picasso's left dons a cigarette
And it is hopeful. He made women solemn and infinite,
though fractured careening from his stroke. Hopeful stroke.
I am a left-handed man. These fingers have no logic
in their need, and desire is a curse. The stroke. Realizing
he couldn't exact their beauty, did he turn his back,
crack a mirror, paint the lines their reflections cast?
Who knows how art is born. You have abandoned me
for sleep and this is what I am left: a room
the color of your sleep. In this darkness I imagine
his *Sleeping Woman With Shutters*. I saw it in a book:
the sad irregular head lowered on her arm, the left hand
touching a blue circular breast. Your left hand touches
my chest and it is perhaps only *coincidence*,
that American word for *fate*. Fate. I have tied fate
to everything, to your body and it is a blessing. Even now,
when you are still as a woman posing for a painting.

The painter strokes that stillness onto a canvas,
hopes his hand can give it breath. I am only as blessed
as a man bound to his desire; to lines that cannot deliver
or mimic life. I am only as hopeless; closing these fingers
around your wrist as it sleeps upon my chest.

STILL MUSIC

"Reminiscence of the Tempyo Era" Ishibashi Museum of Art, Japan

How long til this water evaporates?
　　　There is rain & beauty everywhere
Tonight. Hanging from the train straps,

Nodding with exhaust in the seats.
　　　Women in with wet scarves
& hair, faces which have grown,

These last months, more beautiful
　　　To me. Last week I saw a woman
From the Tempyo Era hanging without a name

On a museum's wall, a strange string
　　　Instrument held in her hands
The way the neck held her face. Still music.

There are tunnels guiding each note
　　　Tonight, these women's murmurs,
Soft, indiscernible, away from me.

What do you call desire in a married man?
　　　Women's bodies shine
In the buttons on my coat. Women lean

From the train straps above me,
　　　Women are anchored
To the seats. The rain falls as if to wash

Away their stations of fatigue.
　　　I know nothing about this place,
But, Wife, tonight I don't want to sleep.

I want to rise into your lungs,
      Linger like a music in your throat,
Vanish like water under heat.

IV. A Gram of &s

g a n d e r

When the girl near
you uncrosses her legs, you glimpse a garden

over the Nabokov you're read-
ing. In the time it takes to slow drag your aged
& steadily aging eyeball from one corner to another, a gear
rolls onto the dance floor of the heart's grand
hotel. Blood begins to sluice & rage

in the cells & rooms & closets until you are reduced to a grade-
school blush. All the questions you wouldn't dare
ask. It must be the book: Humbert's danger-
ous poison passion. *Dear* you mutter. *Dear. Dear. O Dear.*

g e n e r a l

The eager-
ness of a man the War doesn't near.

A leer
straight out of the John Wayne genre.

An eagle
blazing on his brim & breastplate, his useless battle gear.

If he's not there, how will his men learn
the eighty-four methods used to turn anger

into the angle
of light on a blade? Into the Angel

of Light on a blade? Into a gnarl & glare?

m a s c u l i n e

The word some dudes claim came
first. Delved from the plus & minus
system God used to slice
open Himself. Or the smile
of old deacons in the Amen
corner during the part of the Easter Musical
where Mary Magdalene has to clean
the feet of Jesus to beat a stint in Hell. And the malice
in the Angel of Mercy. And the mean
streak in your father's work belt. The gram of vein & muscle
that tipped Babylon's scale.

n u c l e a r

How to make a nation say,   *uncle*.
In other words: how to rule.
We learn
there will be no clue
before it happens.   No clear
sign from the Cosmos.   A clan-
destine airplane will appear   wrapped in the lace
of a black dream. Then a flash   like an ulcer
bursting in God's gut.   Citizens who goggle & race
about the city   as the sky becomes a caul-
dron.   The bones burn clean.

o v e r s e a s

I traveled so far west it became east again, over
the mountains & through the woods until mountains rose
again. I knew no one & knew no one would save
me. I learned to savor
the soft pink flesh of fish & listen to the odd verse
whispered by my stooped eaves-
dropping neighbor, a shy woman obliged to serve
green tea from a stout yellow vase.
All the squatting made my knees sore.
I moved with the ease
of an ink stain on a white kimono in a skin I couldn't erase.

p r e f a c e

Well, ain't your mouth a pretty little pace-
maker. And *mmmm* that tongue is a carp
I'd sure like to harpoon! We could eat crêpe-
suzettes in the dim café
below your hypothalamus. I'd pull the last pear
from the pear tree. We could peer
over the ridge of your throat or creep
down the ladder until we reached the reef.
But before setting forth, you should accept whatever's free
because, Baby, I've got at least an acre
of desires you can reap.

r e p a i d

"By the seventeenth year of mortgage your eyes are pried
permanently open. There will be, of course, those moments of Rapid
Eye Movement, the scent of ripe
misfortunes being aired
each month when the paycheck arrives. But no bank would dare
admit that the more you stash the more they raid.
Wealth is founded only on the idea
of wealth. The palm is not a book that should be read
but shut. (My dad told me this & sighed.) The only permanence is the steady drip
of debt. When you pay them, Son, relish the split second of pride
before the mule throws you from the ride."

s a i n t l y

What the Bible said. A satin
cassock. A tail
that never drags in the dirt. No nasty
acne. No yellowed armpit stain.
& no nails
in the hands & feet. No salt
in the wound. Just satiny
sanity. No narrow slit
to stick the tongue through. No tiny
pin pecks for eyes. No last
minute pleas to be added to the list.

s e g r e g a t e

On the first morning of school there is a young tree-
frog waiting patiently at the front gate.
Since this means there will be no classes for the rest
of the day, the children dump their school gear
in their lockers & hustle to the windows to stare.
The girls are eager to transform him with a kiss; the boys eager
to see him on the basketball court. But their principal greets
him with a "Get the Hell out of here!" A security guard fetches the tear-
gas. Some of the older teachers crowd in the doorway like befuddled geese.
"You belong in our swamps not our schools!" they rage.
But clearly the cool-blooded Amphibian-American does not agree.

s t u p o r

Because sooner or later it will all go sour,
the two of you whipped by the sport
of high-ball & boogie, that *Don't stop
til you get enough* rhythm reduced to a spot
on the tongue. Love or anger might sprout
from her throat & worse than the waters of Port
Hangover will be your need to tour
her face for some sort
of *Oh-never-mind-last-night's-spur-
of-the-moment-sex* expression. Drunk or not, Boy, let the spurt
of cold water pour-
ing from her bathroom spigot, slap you awake like a strap.

t o e n a i l s

They can be shellacked to shine like satin.
They can steal
the light of Tinsel
Town. A woman moseying down the aisle
of a supermarket. Their gleam isn't
lost
in the dark nest
of a shoe. Each toe holds a slate
upon which a lover's note
is written. Or each toe is a window his nose
is pressed into.

V. The Law of Falling & Catching Up

FIRE

It was not smoke rising from the mouth
of a woman in search of her daughter,
nor the straw slipper left on the trampled path

that I remembered. I saw nothing.
Hair covered my eyes, & in the dream
I could not close my mouth. Mostly

it smelled of salt and the diligence
of shipbuilders. Occasionally, I'd hear
my brother groan beneath my footsteps.

There was the calm & discretion
of giving up. The roof.
Boards yielding sap and splinters.

My mother was a dark red head wrap.
Her life had been heavier
than the fire she carried on her back.

This is the meaning of the past, Boy.
There were maps & scriptures
carved into my palms, whole towns

I entered sleeping. But I was not hungry,
I remember. My mother turned her tears to rice
& as long as she wept, there was food.

GUN/WOMAN/SON

His mother stands & pries the slug
from her brain. It's 1952. A bloodstain
crawls in sunlight down the wall,
glass melts on the floor. She shifts
the baby, my father, to her clean side
& drops the bullet in the ashtray beside her pipe.
The shooter runs, his gun shucked into high grass
like a crow with no beak. She looks
through the broken window catching the scent
of pine straw and clay . . . *all my life here*
& I never noticed . . . My father doesn't stir beneath
freckles of blood that will brown
by the time the blanket swaddles me,
but his face is twisted on the one dream
infants bring to the world. In it there is a river,
an oarsman with breasts, Indian-gray hair bound
by a red bow. His mother's wound
is a veil of roses. She turns from the window
holding her face in one hand, my daddy
in the other. There is no sheriff in this county.
I appear in the guise of an old farmer;
kiss the tip of her nose & place my father
in a peach basket. The day is ending,
the gunman halfway to Atlanta
with a satchel of hope. My father & I,
we just wait for the train. By Sunday we will be
different people. I will wake in the basket
saying, *Daddy, tell me again how I was born.*

HEARTTHROB

The music went out of my mother's heart
when the car overheated.
We stood on the interstate, passed up by a herd
of travelers who seemed to hardly
notice a boy or his young mother's broken heel,
her blue dress whipping like a flag. But in my heart
I knew a hero would appear. In my heart
I knew the heat,
would ease & someone among the herd
would stop to help. I didn't think this was a hard
wish to fulfill. My mother would be swept from her heels
by a man with a ten-gallon hat on his head.
We'd be saved by one of those head-
strong heroes who rode into her heart
every Saturday evening with heat
rising from the mouth of his pistol. A herd
of hard-
nosed rustlers would ambush him from the hills
and he'd blast them back to Hell.
Sometimes dinner would overheat
on the stove. Sometimes her head
seemed clouded by the smoke rising from her heart.
Sometimes I heard
gunfire come all night from my mother's room. Hard-
nosed bandits knocked to the hard-
wood floors of saloons. Bandits hustling back into the hills.
All day she lay in bed with a pillow below her head,
her hands resting above her heart,
her body warmed by the heat
of her little black-and-white TV. I heard
her laugh when a villain was killed. I heard
her cheer when the hero softened the town folk's hard-
ships and then rode away. She'd say *I wonder if he'll*

come back someday? He'd vanish just as the other men had
done . . . When our car overheated
that August, the man who came to tow us was not a heart-
throb. The sun refused to set in the distance; there was enough heat
to harden anyone's heart. We'd been heading toward the hills,
my mother told him. She'd heard that was where my father lived.

MOTHER TO SON

He was whole evenings
sometimes & pet names,
he was whole breaths
changing into steam—
we'd never leave
the front seat. I'd straddle him
& the odor was black & new
& someone pushing inside.
The radio dial
was a strip of green light
& his fingers turned
my nipples until the music
eased out of me.
He was a palm full
of tiny deaths, desire
spilling cell by cell
& desire swimming up stream.
He was whole years, Son,
& even at this moment,
he walks through your face . . .
He'd drive me home
& at dawn I'd stand
behind my mother's house
hosing between my thighs.
It was on one of those nights
that you were conceived,
& with me then,
as I fanned my dress
until the water dried.

BLUES PROCESSION
for Uncle Bubba (1953–1985)

Come tomorrow, our car had to be bright
As the preacher's capped teeth.

They'd found my uncle's car bundled
In the arms of a tree;

The gin bottle & windshield cracked,
The flesh like moss clinging to his body . . .

My mother knelt with rag & bucket
To knuckle insects from the grill.

I did not know the detours of grief.
I did not know the detours from grief.

I watched her curse untangling the hose
Noosed around her feet. I watched suds

Slide down the glass like storm clouds
Bound to wreck her somewhere in the week.

FLORIDA

In the black-tiled room,
in the slime-wet apron, I am slicing,

I am fingering tiny muscles
of the soul from the fish,

I am doing as I was told,
dropping gut & bile in the bucket with the head

where the eyes are like marbles
in a doll's face. I am inside the fish

thinking of my cousin, Noon Pie's hips
in the walk-in closet, the sex of cloth

against cloth below Aunt Betty-Joe's
yellowing lace, Lonzo's suits of sharkskin,

their stale wedding bouquet.
I know fish love what blossoms

because they're drawn to the propeller's
bloom. I know fish nibble the corpse

til nothing remains, but bone.
I am thinking of Lonzo's hand cuffed

around my wrist. *You cut off the head
like this* . . . I am made to tremble

by a boom box's treble & bass,
B-boys in swimming trunks & shades

as they walk to the neighborhood lake.
All day they will splash & swallow

the water's charm, as I swallow & splash
through heat, dreaming of my home

too many miles from this state
shaped like a leg gnawed up to the knee.

THE FLAME

Her letters doused, the sticky sap
of *Dear Baby* on my tongue,
her apology, the electric twine of ink
all about to be burned, I crouch
as embers rise bright as maggots
into my face. I am in the back yard
looking at the pyramid of roofs,
the glinting antennae, I am looking at vines
of cable & telephone lines hatched over head
where the night sky seems untouchable,
a place I could only trespass.
I am sixteen, age of blood, age the bravest,
meaning the most desperate, of my crew struts
into class wearing no underwear
& spends the whole day proving it.
I have done this. Felt the rough blue pull
of denim & later, the teeth of sweat,
the embarrassment spawned by too much passion.
Now, only this flame will do.
The neighbors wonder, Who is burning leaves
this time of night? Or worse, Who is weeping
for the burning of leaves? This is called a pyre.
Long ago a tribe would gather articles of the dead:
the socks & Halloween masks, crayons & the child
like a sack of wind. They gathered
whatever was flammable & gave it wings.
They knew what *wasn't* flammable
burned the most. I am learning this tonight.
I am learning the name of all the ballads
& stupid movies, all the world's crushed moping.
And still, none of it will do. The flames gasp,
the pages transformed to what everything becomes
by the end. Tomorrow, perhaps no one will know
if these ashes were leaves or wood,   cloth,   skin.

ODE TO STONE

My child is old as stone
　　　Which does not budge from dirt

Though he will not wake me
　　　Half-naked from my dreams

Though we will not wait for a yellow bus
　　　To climb the hill at dawn

My child is old as the stone
　　　Which sank years ago into the earth

Though he still lies naked in my dreams
　　　Though I say his name at dawn

My child is old as stone
　　　This morning I walk the empty field

This morning I fill my mouth with dirt
　　　From a hill gorged with bones

ALTER CALL

To ask it once & for all
    & for all
        the brains argued out
of the conversation.
      To sleep
in a straight line
    & never be outrage
revealed in a sneeze.
      To mow,
        to snip & prune
the growling in the distance,
    Lord.
To live among the patient,
    the forgiven,
        striking a bell
four thousand times a day.
    To never think
      of one man
as all men.
      But to loosen
the valve on each fury.
    To alter
      the arc of my grin,
my face,
    on its wobbling
      axis. Lord, a parasol
of Your Mercy.
    To rise
    in Your Manor, Lord.
In Your Manner.
      Do I ask too much?
        To know, truly,
what heals

all wounds.
        To rock the coffin
of Death & His concubines.
       To gather the blue stones
            of Imperfection, Lord.
& cast them away.

AUTUMN

Because the leaves ache
& the rush-hour dusk begins
to thicken & slow,
in this, the season of your birth,

your skull's music box begins
its few imperfect notes,
& one of your younger selves
heads North behind a teenaged couple
from the Catholic school,
behind the sway of the girl's plaid skirt
& cape of black braids,
the boy's loose, almost criminal strut—

you follow them through the traffic's caesura,
through the lot of the boarded-up Rite Aid,
the fire station opposite the Burger King
& its jaded daydreaming workers,

its scent of cooling grease
like the scent you inhaled once
along the rim of a girl's collar,
the untangling bun of her hair.

You leaned into each other
in the break room,
doubled in red & black aprons,
your large visors removed,
her tongue held like a moist wing
between your lips—
your foolish self,
your younger, better self,
the one you see in the couple's
lanky, unpolished grace.

You call to them & the sound
of your voice is reduced to a murmur
as you wake in a dim blue room
beside your wife. You want to tell her,

with your whole self,
though the other selves remain
lost, loitering, in love,

how there is a taste
like regurgitated skin or perhaps feathers
in your mouth,
I have had a strange dream,
you want to say,

but because now you can only remember
that you were younger, heading North,
you think it was just a dream about age

& then, instead of waking her,
you, my backward-doubling little self,
awaken me.

THE SAME CITY

The rain falling on a night
    in mid-December,
I pull to my father's engine
    wondering how long I'll remember
this. His car is dead. He connects
    jumper cables to his battery,
then to mine without looking in
    at me & the child. Water beads
on the windshields, the road sign,
    his thin blue coat. I'd get out now,
prove I can stand with him
    in the cold, but he told me to stay
with the infant. I wrap her
    in the blanket staring
for what seems like a long time
    into her open, toothless mouth,
and wish she was mine. I feed her
    an orange softened first in my mouth,
chewed gently until the juice runs
    down my fingers as I squeeze it
into hers. What could any of this matter
    to another man passing on his way
to his family, his radio deafening
    the sound of water & breathing
along all the roads bound to his?
    But to rescue a soul is as close
as anyone comes to God.
    Think of Noah lifting a small black bird
from its nest. Think of Joseph
    raising a son that wasn't his.

Let me begin again.
    I want to be holy. In rain

I pull to my father's car
   with my girlfriend's infant.
She was pregnant when we met.
   But we'd make love. We'd make
love below stars & shingles
   while the baby kicked between us.
Perhaps a man whose young child
   bears his face, whose wife waits
as he drives home through rain
   & darkness, perhaps that man
would call me a fool. So what.
   There is one thing I will remember
all my life. It is as small
   & holy as the mouth
of an infant. It is speechless.
   When his car would not stir,
my father climbed in beside us,
   took the orange from my hand,
took the baby in his arms.
   In 1974, this man met my mother
for the first time as I cried or slept
   in the same city that holds us
tonight. If you ever tell my story,
   say that's the year I was born.

for James L. Hayes

NOTES

"LORDE"

The poem is made up of whole and partial lines in the index (under W) of *The Collected Poems of AUDRE LORDE*.

A GRAM OF &S

The poems are based on the daily word game found in the puzzle section of many syndicated newspapers. I end each line with one of the eleven words derived from the title word, while abiding by the other rules of the game: 1. Words must be derived from four or more letters. 2. Words that acquire four letters by the addition of "s," such as "bats" or "dies" are not used. 3. Only one form of a verb is used.

"BROKEN DANGERFIELD NEWBY VILLANELLE"

The poem is inspired by the death of Dangerfield Newby, one of the five black men involved in John Brown's raid on Harper's Ferry. Newby had joined Brown as a last hope to free his wife and six children from slavery. He was the first killed.

ACKNOWLEDGMENTS

Sincerest gratitude to the people associated with the publications in which most of the poems in this collection first appeared (sometimes in different versions):

art/life; The Beloit Poetry Journal; The Bloomsbury Review; Callaloo; Chelsea; Controlled Burn; Crab Orchard Review; failbetter.com; 5 am; incontext.com; Indiana Review; Harvard Review; The Journal; Luna; New Orleans Review; Paterson Literary Review; The Pittsburgh Quarterly; Ploughshares; Red Brick Review; River City; The Southern Review; Wind; Xavier Review.

"Florida" appeared in the 1999 Chester H. Jones Foundation Anthology of National Competition Winners.

"For Paul Robeson" also appeared in the 1999 Cave Canem Anthology.

"The Things-No-One-Knows Blues" also appeared in the 2000 Cave Canem Anthology.

"Heartthrob" was originally published as "Heroic Sestina" in The Bloomsbury Review.

"For Robert Hayden," "Squawk," and "For Paul Robeson" also appeared in Speak the Truth to the People, NOMMO Literary Anthology.

Deepest love and appreciation to Yona Harvey and Joel Dias Porter (aka DJ Renegade) for their indispensable scrutiny and support during the completion of this manuscript; and to Shara McCallum for her unwavering friendship and encouragement. Thanks also to the writing communities of Cave Canem and the NOMMO Literary Society of New Orleans. Finally, a special thanks goes to Cornelius Eady for selecting this manuscript.